An Analysis of Internal Auditing Internships

Glenn E. Sumners, DBA, CPA, CFE
Rodger G. Holland, PhD
Kimberley Klass
Louisiana State University

The Institute of Internal Auditors Research Foundation

Disclosure

ISBN 0-89413-307-1
93212 02/94
First Printing

Contents

Page

Acknowledgments vii
Introduction 1
Benefits to the Profession 3
Benefits to the University 5
Benefits to the Student 7
- Educational Benefits 7
- Learning Experience 7
- Compensation and Credit 7
- CIA Exam 8
- Career Placement 8
- Human Relations 9
- Miscellaneous 9

Benefits to the Organization 11
Internship Structure 13
- Goals and Objectives 13
- Policies and Procedures 13
- Budgetary Process 14
- Time Frame 15
- Selection Process 16
- Mentors 17
- Orientation 17
- Transition 18
- Related Activities 18

Intern Selection 19
On-site Campus Visit 21
Follow-up 23
Office Visit 25
Classroom Follow-up 27
Academic Impact of Internships 29
- Introduction 29
- Post-internship Evaluations 30

Executive Summary of Summer Internship Questionnaires 33
Conclusion 45
Appendices 47
- Appendix A: Summer Internship Survey: Student Evaluation by Sponsor (Form E) 47

Appendix B: Summer Internship Survey - Student Report (Form S) 51
Appendix C: Louisiana State University Internal Auditing Internship Program – Post-internship Evaluation 59
Appendix D: The Institute of Internal Auditors Endorsed Internal Auditing Programs 61
References 65
Organizations 67

List of Tables

Page

Table 1 30
Post-internship Evaluations

Table 2 34
Mean Scores of Items and Correlations with Evaluations: Sorted by Mean Scores

Table 3 35
Mean Scores of Items and Correlations with Evaluations: Sorted by Correlations with Pre-internship Evaluations

Table 4 36
Mean Scores of Items and Correlations with Evaluations: Sorted by Correlations with Post-internship Evaluations

Table 5 38
Means by Ancillary Class Variables
(Permanent Employment Decision)

Table 6 39
Means by Ancillary Class Variables
(Interest in Permanent Employment)

Table 7 39
Means by Ancillary Class Variables
(Discussion of Evaluations)

Table 8 41
Professional Qualifications Ranked by Means

Table 9 42
Performance Qualifications Ranked by Means

Table 10 43
Personal Qualifications Ranked by Means

Table 11 44
Responses to Questions 5 – 12
(Form E, Appendix A)

Acknowledgments

This study is dedicated to the many practitioners who have sponsored internal auditing internships over the years. Such participation has helped further internal auditing education, particularly in The IIA's Endorsed Internal Auditing Programs. This involvement contributes to the growth of the profession and encourages students to consider challenging careers in internal auditing.

Introduction

Internship programs are designed to give students practical experience in their chosen profession before they complete their academic work. This "hands-on" learning experience supplements the textbook-driven education process and often brings about a deeper understanding and lasting benefit for everyone involved. Many organizations view the internship process as a unique way to make contact with students and create a presence on campus. First of all, it is a good opportunity to inform students about the career potential and challenges that the internal auditing profession has to offer. Secondly, internal auditing has historically not had significant textbook exposure, and an internship program provides an excellent accompaniment to the classroom and the career decision process.

The Institute of Internal Auditors (IIA) Research Foundation is creating a data base of 100 organizations that are interested in sponsoring an internal auditing internship. This data base will be especially beneficial to The IIA's Endorsed Internal Auditing Programs and schools with structured internship programs. The data base will facilitate the entire internship process by improving the communication among sponsors, schools, and students.

Though internship programs are as diverse as the students that participate in them, they can be a crucial part of the internal auditing education process if structured properly. By investing in such programs, universities, students, organizations, and the internal auditing profession share in the short-term and long-term returns. Internships are an important way to support The IIA's motto, "Progress Through Sharing."

Internship programs have historically been supported as a beneficial part of the education process. For example, in 1952 the American Accounting Association's (AAA) Committee on Internship Programs concluded that internships enhance an understanding of the business world, provide exposure to business problems that are not included in textbooks, and enhance students' ability to absorb academic knowledge. For these reasons, the AAA encouraged the wider adoption of internship programs. In 1956 the Commission on Standards of Education and Experience for Certified Public Accountants issued "Standards of Education and Experience for CPAs," which recommended internship programs as part of the professional training for CPAs. In 1969 the AICPA Beamer Committee Report recommended internships as a part of the education process and to add meaning to subsequent courses. In 1987 the AICPA's "Report of the Committee on Education and Experience Requirements for CPAs" encouraged the formation of internships. More recently, in 1987, the National Commission on Fraudulent Financial Reporting concluded that, "The most serious deficiency in attempts to improve the business curriculum along the lines the Commission recommends is the lack of relevant classroom discussions of real situations and of challenging classroom materials." To some extent, an internship program addresses these concerns.

Many schools currently offer internship programs. The 1991 Survey of Internal Auditing Education identified 28 schools with structured internship programs in internal audit, and other schools have generic programs. In addition, many students at schools without formal internship programs are interested in internships. With a tight job market, networking through internships becomes even more important in hiring decisions.

This report is designed to inform readers about the significant benefits provided by an internship program. We accept the objective of an internship program as the development of superior entry-level internal auditors, thus resulting in benefits to the student, the profession, the university, and the organization. To best accomplish this objective, internship programs must be structured to provide students with relevant experience.

The report examines the structure of an internship program from the perspective of the sponsoring organization as well as the university. Information is also provided on the sources of interns, the campus visit, the office visit, and the follow-up process. A properly developed internship program can have a profound academic impact, which the report also addresses. Finally, the report presents the results of eight years of data gathered from students and organizations participating in the Louisiana State University's (LSU) summer internship program. At the conclusion of the internship, students and sponsoring organizations complete in-depth questionnaires. Throughout this report the data analysis is referred to as "the LSU questionnaires." The information may prove useful in providing future direction for internship programs.

Benefits to the Profession

A properly designed internship program is a system for early communication between students and practicing internal auditors and a valuable method of attracting top students into the profession. The future of the profession depends on improving the quality of input into the profession and internships provide a means of accomplishing this. The Institute of Internal Auditors supports internships through its Endorsed Internal Auditing Programs. Interestingly, 98 percent of the practitioners that participate in LSU's internship program feel that The IIA should aggressively encourage internal auditing education at colleges and universities. These questionnaires are presented as Appendices A and B and provide the data used in the tables throughout this report.

Internal auditing is a relatively new profession, particularly in relation to public accounting. Internships contribute to the visibility of the profession on campus, thus presenting internal auditing to the students as a viable career alternative. The internship program is an opportunity to identify and directly attract students to the profession. Following the internships, students return enthusiastic about and with an appreciation for internal auditing. They tend to view internal auditing as a dynamic, maturing profession, an outlook they might not have had before their internship. This has positive effects on how other students view internal auditing as a profession and as a career possibility.

The profession traditionally has relied primarily upon the secondary markets for entry-level personnel. The internship program facilitates the development of an alternative source of personnel by attracting the fresh talent of college students. Interns often add a unique perspective to old issues, and sometimes their inquisitive questions can lead to a reexamination of accepted practices that need revamping. By providing endorsed programs with internships, organizations can lend credibility and status to these programs, thus helping to ensure their success and the success of the profession. These programs help build communication between industry and academia which over the long term will produce students who are better suited for the workplace.

Benefits to the University

The main direct benefit that the university receives from an internal auditing internship program is the contribution that the program makes to the education of the students. Many subjects, particularly those relating to auditing, cannot be totally mastered in a classroom as it is often difficult for students to visualize certain processes and transaction flows. The internship is a viable and meaningful supplement to traditional classroom instruction. It also enhances classroom learning for other students subsequent to the internship, as interns share their experiences during classroom discussions. Students tend to listen more to their fellow students than to their professors. Their input can be used to amplify the importance of various skills.

When the intern returns to school, classes have more relevance and purpose as the student realizes how course work fits in with actual practice. As a result of the practical experience, students are better able to understand what is being communicated to them in the classroom, resulting in improved academic performance particularly in auditing courses. Internships also provide students with the ability to select courses to improve those areas where weaknesses were identified through the internship. Students must compete for the best internships, just as they later must compete for the best jobs. By moving this competition up, students start paying closer attention to classroom performance earlier.

Universities also benefit from the cooperative relationship that internship programs foster with the practitioners and the profession. In one survey, over 90 percent of the respondents felt that the internship program increased cooperation and understanding between practitioners and members of the faculty (Lowe, 1965). During an internship, the student has the opportunity to put into practice the knowledge obtained in the classroom, thus allowing the intern to better judge the quality of classes being offered. By securing corporate support of the program, the university can identify the changing needs of the business world and structure curricula to meet these needs. If universities can better prepare graduates for their careers, the quality of education increases. Increased educational quality results in better placement of graduates. As a consequence, the university attracts higher caliber students and gains respect in the academic community.

Benefits to the Student

Educational Benefits

Internship programs can provide a number of educational benefits to the student by enhancing and supplementing classroom education. Research related to this area is subsequently discussed in the "Academic Impact of Internships" chapter.

Learning Experience

Internships offer students the opportunity to investigate and learn about the internal auditing function. Interns are treated as professionals (often for the first time) who have their own assignments and responsibilities. Internships expose students to the business environment and all the human factors involved. This kind of experience cannot be easily replicated in a classroom setting. In addition to seeing first-hand how an organization functions, students are exposed to the corporate culture of an organization and learn the corporate jargon and the importance of a professional attitude. Students also benefit from the flexibility and freedom to meet, learn from, and work with people at all levels of the organization.

Internships provide students with a realistic view of the internal auditing function as well as the information they need to make a more intelligent career decision. Not only can students determine if the internal auditing profession fits their needs and personality, they can also develop a feel for an industry and a geographical location. Such exposure to "real life" experiences may confirm a career choice or lead to another selection. Alternatively, the student may decide that internal auditing in a particular industry is not an area in which to begin a career. It is more cost-effective for students to find out during an internship that they do not like a given position, industry, or organization than to find out after accepting a permanent position. Furthermore, interns have less turnover and higher job satisfaction than students who did not participate in an internship.

The transition from the classroom to the work environment is not always an easy one. An internship eases a student into the profession, which makes the transition process a little smoother. Students gain insight into the profession and the reality of work demands on a professional so that there are fewer surprises when they permanently enter the profession.

Compensation and Credit

Most internal auditing internships offer compensation to the student which varies by industry, location, and organization. On average, many organizations target the compensation at approximately 80 percent of a new hire. Many students have financial obligations for tuition and living expenses and cannot accept an internship without compensation. Such compensation is usually more than a student could earn at most other summer jobs, and the student benefits from learning about a profession he or she is interested in pursuing. The lower salary also allows organizations to recoup training costs in a short time.

Many internal auditing internships also offer college credit. The amount of credit varies by university; however, for 10 to 12 weeks of full-time work a student usually receives three semester credit hours.

CIA Exam

Internships in internal auditing help a student prepare for the Certified Internal Auditor (CIA) exam. A portion of the CIA exam is practical in nature and is difficult for students who do not have benefit of relevant work experience. The internship provides some of the auditing knowledge necessary for the exam, thus reducing the need for full-time experience. Even though the exam is structured for a person with two years of experience, an internship in tandem with an internal auditing course can reduce the amount of experience necessary to pass the exam. Many of the CIA Student High Achievement Award winners attribute their success in part to their internship experience.

The internship also furnishes a share of the internal auditing experience required for the CIA designation. The work experience of an intern typically counts toward that required to become certified.

Career Placement

Internships provide experience, compensation, and college credit, but they also supply the intern with the knowledge to make a more intelligent career decision. It is not unusual for a student to be nearing graduation and still be uncertain about the future. The internship provides clarification of career objectives by giving students a better idea of what they want to do after graduation.

In a tight job market, even students with the most glowing grade point averages may have difficulty getting a job without some practical experience. Students with lower grade point averages are at a particular disadvantage in hard economic times. An outstanding performance during an internship can help a student overcome other disadvantages such as a modest grade point average or lack of extracurricular activities.

Networking is particularly important when the job market is tight. An internship gives a student the opportunity to interact with professionals, thus facilitating professional development. Contacts made during an internship can be valuable while searching for a permanent position as well as during the student's professional career.

A permanent job offer is often extended by the sponsoring organization following the internship. However, even if a permanent position does not materialize with the sponsoring organization, the student has an important resume item as well as a reference(s) for other positions. The intern will also have some experience in interviewing, which should provide a competitive advantage during the recruiting process.

Once a student has accepted a permanent position with an organization, his or her performance should be superior to other new hires who did not take advantage of an internship. Interns have more internal auditing experience and are more comfortable in a professional environment than students without internship experience. Students who have the opportunity to participate in an internship program will derive many benefits when beginning their permanent employment search.

Human Relations

Good interpersonal skills which are necessary for success in internal auditing are not easily learned in college courses. Internships give students the chance to develop interpersonal skills through the interview process, participation in meetings, working in groups, and giving presentations. By working as a team member, interns develop listening skills and sensitivity to others, as well as conflict resolution skills. Written communication proficiency is also developed as the intern prepares working papers, memos, and reports.

Miscellaneous

Advice from experienced internal auditors is helpful to students who are preparing to enter the profession. Input from other staff members about their experiences and tips about interviewing or preparing for certification exams are also beneficial. If students capitalize on the opportunity to interface with people in the profession, the intangible benefits of an internship will exceed the tangibles such as compensation and credit.

Although interns work hard during their internships, they also have a lot of fun. Some organizations hold social activities such as banquets, receptions, and picnics that interns have the opportunity to attend. Another advantage is the possibility of travel, perhaps even internationally. An internship is a great time for students to decide whether they enjoy the lifestyle of an internal auditing professional. If not, it is better to discover this during an internship than after accepting a permanent position.

An internship is an excellent way to begin one's career. It is not very often that a college student can learn about the profession, gain experience, receive university credit, earn money, and travel all in the same summer.

Benefits to the Organization

A properly designed internship program can be an integral recruiting tool for a sponsoring organization. A quality program attracts some of the brightest students by increasing university and student awareness of opportunities in internal auditing. When the opportunity presents itself, many interns accept employment from their sponsoring organizations after graduation. Additionally, a student returning from an internship with a favorable impression becomes on-campus advertisement and contributes to the organization's presence on campus. Students listen to their peers and trust their opinions more than those of campus representatives or professors. The cost of recruiting permanent employees is reduced as students become familiar with the opportunities the organization has to offer and top students are attracted to permanent positions.

Internships often result in an improved selection process for permanent employees. Organizations are able to evaluate students who might otherwise not be considered. For example, many students have certain qualities that offset relatively poor grade point averages, but the question remains concerning technical competence. It is difficult to directly compare students who work while going to school against those who do not. Other difficult comparisons involve officers of student organizations who have devoted significant effort to those endeavors which may impact grades. Organizations may take the risk of offering a relatively low-cost internship and end up discovering hidden talents.

During the internship the organization has the opportunity to observe the student at work and review work habits, technical ability, personality, interpersonal skills, and adaptability before making a full-time commitment. The information that can be obtained about an intern during a three-month period could not be obtained from a resume, transcript, or even a series of interviews. This substantially minimizes the risk should an offer of permanent employment be made because it is less expensive to hire an intern in error than to hire that same person on a permanent basis. Not only does the organization have the opportunity to pre-screen the intern, but the student can also learn about the organization. This will help alleviate the problem of employee turnover as students will be more familiar with the future position and less likely to be dissatisfied with it, resulting in a better match of employer and employee.

The internal auditing department can obtain qualified personnel at reasonable cost with an internship program. The responsibilities and work that an internal auditing intern performs are the same as that of an entry-level auditor, yet the department may not have to permanently increase staff size or pay benefits. Interns can satisfy seasonal needs and short-term staffing requirements or assist with special projects that are suitable to their academic background and experience level. Interns are often enthusiastic about learning and offer creative new ideas or perspectives which contribute to the completion of audit work or the solving of problems. Since they are often trying to obtain a permanent offer, they may work even harder than new hires.

Organizations can use the internship as a training period for a student who may later join them on a permanent basis. However, the internship also enhances the development of the auditing staff by requiring training and supervision of an intern. Internships challenge managers and supervisors by forcing an evaluation and organization of their own duties and responsibilities. Managers and supervisors will be more aware of their own actions, and such self-reflections can lead to improvements in operations or procedures.

The internship process is an opportunity for organizations to develop and maintain relations with universities, while gaining exposure on campus. Good relations with universities provide organizations with opportunities to communicate their needs, thus potentially influencing the education process. Camaraderie between an organization and faculty ensures that the best students are recommended to the organization.

Participation in an internship program demonstrates an organization's commitment to improving the quality of the profession. The image of the internal auditing profession is enhanced through increased communication with students and faculty, resulting in an increased importance of all internal auditing departments. There is greater recognition of the importance of internal auditing work if management feels the organization has benefited from the internship process. In the long run, the greatest benefit of the internship program is the organization's ability to professionally develop a future permanent employee.

Internship Structure

Goals and Objectives

Before notifying the university that an internship is available, an organization should establish goals and objectives for the program. This ensures that everyone involved is aware of the educational nature of the program. The internship should supplement classroom instruction by focusing on areas of internal auditing practice that are not available in school or that tie theory to practice. The student gains some practical experience in internal auditing, while developing maturity and confidence. To summarize some earlier points, the sponsoring organization may also want to include the following objectives in the internship program:

- Fill critical productivity needs without having to hire full-time personnel.
- Promote internal auditing as a career choice for college graduates.
- Create a trial period during which the organization and the student can evaluate each other.
- Serve as a recruiting tool.
- Provide input for course work.
- Gain fresh perspectives and new ideas.
- Demonstrate commitment to improving the quality of the profession.

The development of formal goals and objectives helps to focus the efforts of all involved parties and provides for a clear understanding of what the program is designed to accomplish.

Policies and Procedures

The success of the internship program depends on commitment from all parties. Before the intern arrives, the organization should establish policies and procedures to address the needs and roles of all key players. Managers should consider conducting a training session to cover the requirements and the overall purpose of the internship program. Below are some issues that need to be addressed regarding policies and procedures.

A coordinator for the internship program should be chosen. This person interacts with the student, human resources, the university, and faculty advisor. The coordinator is responsible for administrative duties such as the preemployment physical, orientation, and paperwork.

A job description is important because it sets the compliance standard for the student, the organization, and the university. The job description should include an explanation of the objectives, the student's responsibilities, the reporting structure, and what the student should be expected to learn from the experience. The knowledge, education, and skills required should also be included. Many organizations use their new-hire job descriptions for their internship program. The organization must ensure that the student has a clear understanding of work rules and standards of professional conduct.

Student interns require adequate supervision. This is critical to obtaining maximum benefits, both from the intern's perspective and the organization's. A successful intern supervisor should have strong instructional skills and be patient as the intern grows professionally. The supervisor must make an extra effort to assist the student in developing creative, strategic, interpersonal, and technical skills.

The coordinator should decide in advance what specific types of work will be assigned to the intern. The students will not be experienced enough to do certain tasks, however, they should be challenged. A student that is continually assigned clerical duties will likely become bored and form a negative impression, and the potential gains may become liabilities. Reasonable expectations should be set for what the intern can accomplish during the internship period. Students should be provided with varied assignments in order to learn as much as possible during their short stay. If possible, interns should also have the opportunity to see audits progress from the planning stages to the issuance of the report.

Management should evaluate the intern, discuss progress, and offer advice on professional development. The intern should also be given the opportunity to discuss any problems and concerns. Given the temporary status of interns, they can be more direct and candid than new hires if employers are willing to take steps to solicit their opinions. If possible, the organization should provide the intern with feedback on performance following each auditing assignment to allow time to work on deficiencies. If credit is granted, two reports should be completed at the conclusion of the internship and submitted to the faculty advisor. One report is the organization's evaluation of the student. The organization is encouraged to share the evaluation with the student, however, they are not obligated to do so. The second report is the student's evaluation of the internship program. The student should have the option of sharing this report with the organization. Some organizations may require a student to complete additional evaluations or to participate in an exit conference as a way to critique their program and make any necessary improvements.

Interns should be treated as professional staff personnel. They should read current professional articles and attend and participate in staff meetings. Offering the intern student membership in The IIA (if the intern is not already a member) is another way to make the intern feel like a part of the profession. Formal policies and procedures are necessary if students are to receive the maximum benefit from the experience.

Budgetary Process

Before deciding to sponsor an intern the organization must determine how much they are willing to invest in establishing the program. The cost/benefit considerations are similar to those for a new hire. In addition to student compensation, the internship will incur costs in terms of training, development, and supervision. The organization must determine the length of the internship program and the number of interns that should be hired. The number is dependent on the experience the organization has in managing a program, the available budget and space, the number of people on staff who are available to supervise interns, and their staffing needs. Unless the department has discretionary payroll funds, the program will require budgetary approval and endorsement from senior management, as is the case with any newly created position.

Although many students would consider the opportunity to obtain relevant work experience as adequate compensation, most are not financially able to work full-time for eight to 12 weeks while earning no income. Offering reasonable compensation will convince most potential interns of the value of the program. An organization can contact the faculty advisor, the placement office, and peers to find out what compensation is considered appropriate.

Most organizations do not pay for the relocation and housing expenses incurred by interns. However, many interns incur significant travel, housing, and relocation costs in order to accept an internship. An organization can improve its chances of attracting high quality interns by covering a portion of these costs or assisting students in minimizing their expenses.

The organization must also ensure that there is sufficient office space for the intern. There should be ample work space with a telephone and, if necessary, a personal computer. Providing an office or cubicle, if available, should help the intern feel like a part of the staff.

Time Frame

The best time frame for an internship varies depending on work load, available supervision, and hiring philosophy. Many organizations prefer to have continuous assistance and hire interns throughout the year. Others prefer a specified time of the year to coincide with a quarter or semester school year. The decision is also influenced by the number of interns hired. For example, a sponsor may hire four interns for the same time frame. An organization can target schools that have internship programs that correspond with their internship needs. For efficiency and effectiveness, all four students could coordinate on all aspects of the internship process (administration, orientation, evaluation, etc.)

The Survey identified the following time frames for schools with structured internal auditing internships:

7 - Spring.

12 - Summer.

5 - Fall.

13 - Throughout the year.

1 - Winter quarter.

It is often more efficient for the university to offer the internship program just once per year. Faculty coordination of an internship program can be extremely time consuming if the faculty advisor is involved in the pre-screening, scheduling, sponsor hosting, and selection process. Sixty-one percent of the schools surveyed granted credit for the internship.

From the student's perspective, an internship offers many advantages over a co-op program. While the co-op provides more financial assistance, the internship program may not delay or will not significantly delay the graduation date. Other than financial considerations, the internship typically provides most of the same benefits.

Selection Process

The criteria that most sponsoring organizations use in selecting interns is similar, if not identical, to that used in selecting permanent personnel. This is logical since many organizations use the internship program as a recruiting tool for hiring permanent employees. In general, the organization should pursue the best match between their needs and what a prospective intern has to offer. This should satisfy both the organization and the student.

The student's major course of study should be evaluated, giving consideration to what type of work he or she will be expected to perform. For example, if the intern position focuses primarily on financial auditing, an accounting or finance major may be desired. Alternatively, if the focus is information systems auditing, an intern with a more technical background such as computer science may be appropriate. Grade point average, previous experience, and extracurricular activities are areas that are traditionally given attention. The student's status in the program of study may be important to some employers, particularly if the department has a policy pertaining to education requirements. For example, some organizations require or prefer students with graduate degrees and others prefer an undergraduate. In internal auditing it is important for a student to be willing to travel; and in today's global economy, foreign language skills are definitely a plus.

During the selection process the organization should also seek students who display characteristics that, though less tangible, are nevertheless important in determining success. Some of these traits include interest and involvement in the profession, positive thinking, enthusiasm, adherence to deadlines, commitment, drive, loyalty, and perceptiveness. Obviously, one skill coveted by recruiters is the ability to solve unstructured problems. Successful interns should also possess good interpersonal and leadership skills. Above all, the prospective intern must be a good personal match with the culture of the organization.

Sponsors are provided with five general alternatives in selecting an intern. First, the organizations may visit the placement center on campus and conduct interviews. Second, resumes may be reviewed and office visits may be scheduled for selected students. Third, the organization may simply select a candidate from the resumes. Fourth, selection may be completed through telephone interviews. Finally, selection may be based solely upon the recommendation of the faculty advisor. Respondents to the LSU questionnaires were asked to respond to the following question:

What type of interviewing format do you prefer?

48%	On-campus interview.
29%	On campus with selected office visits.
8%	Office visits only.
11%	Faculty recommendations.
4%	Review of resumes.

The percentages reflect the respondents' first choice. Interestingly, 89 percent of the respondents had multiple responses to this question.

An organization should use the method that suits its purposes, including any combination of the alternatives. The selection process should be effective so that both the sponsoring organization and the student receive the maximum benefit.

Mentors

One mutually beneficial arrangement for the internship program is a mentor approach. This type of relationship benefits not only the intern but also the mentor. Many organizations that have structured programs assign mentors to interns and new hires. Some people fill the mentor role quite naturally while others struggle. Natural (unassigned) mentoring usually leads to informal identification of those most suited for this role and builds stronger relationships. However, such informal relationships may not develop quickly enough for the rapid pace of an internship so the structured approach is often necessary. The only disadvantage of a structured program is that the right "chemistry" may not develop between the matched mentor and the intern. The internship coordinator should monitor this process and make reassignments as needed.

Interns typically gain a broader and more in-depth perspective when issues are explained by a mentor who is interested in their progress. The mentor and intern should informally meet in a non-business setting (coffee break, lunch, etc.) to discuss problems, concerns, and professional growth. Mentors are able to communicate without the intern feeling judged or evaluated.

The mentor/intern relationship is widespread due to the mutual benefits. Regardless of the formality or informality of the program, the relationship should be an integral part of every organization's internship program.

Orientation

When practical, the organization should provide some standardized training before the intern assumes any auditing responsibility. This orientation phase should be formally planned and should be similar to that presented to a new hire. Some of the specifics such as insurance and benefits need not be covered, but an intern can learn a great deal and function more effectively if he or she is given a basic introduction. The intern should be exposed to some basic company terminology and culture as well as the organization's operations and internal auditing policies and procedures.

The length of the orientation can last anywhere from one day to a week or more. At a minimum it should include tours of various departments, meetings with key personnel, and a review of the policy manual, the code of conduct, and the standard operating procedure manual. Organizations must keep in mind that many issues that seem obvious to the seasoned employee must be explained to the intern. Providing the intern with a solid introduction will reduce the risk of any misunderstanding later.

Training programs are designed to foster the efficiency and effectiveness of the auditing staff and the intern should be included in this process. By providing an intern with a proper orientation, he or she will be better prepared to perform quality work, and the chance of becoming a permanent employee increases. If the intern does become a permanent employee, limited training would be required. A quality orientation program will work to the advantage of both the intern and the organization.

Transition

Students accepting internships must often relocate and find a place to live. Their attitude toward the sponsoring organization, as well as toward the internship in general, will be more positive if they are provided with advice and guidance on relocation matters. Providing apartment guides, university dormitory information, and chamber of commerce brochures will assist students in finding a place to live for the duration of the internship. Members of the auditing staff may also be able to contribute some additional insight that will be helpful to interns.

Related Activities

An intern's perception of the internship will be more positive if he or she is given the opportunity to experience the entire professional environment. This includes professional training and development, staff meetings, and travel. The intern should be kept busy and rotated among several assignments in order to learn as much about the organization as possible. Social functions are also an integral part of the internship experience. Interns should be invited to professional meetings (such as local IIA chapter meetings), company picnics, and other after-hours activities.

Intern Selection

How should an organization select interns? Preliminary screening processes might include weighing the differences between accounting versus non-accounting majors, graduate versus undergraduate, and local versus regional or national schools. The criteria for this selection should include economy, efficiency, effectiveness, and past results.

The organization should develop a list of primary schools to target for selecting interns. The local IIA Chapter Academic Relations Chairman can facilitate the recruiting process by providing a link between students, professors, and sponsors. The International Academic Relations Committee (ARC) members can also facilitate the coordination. The Academic Relations Manual of the ARC contains a useful section on internships. Additionally, The IIA's Manager of Academic Relations can serve as a liaison between schools, professors, students, and organizations relative to academic relations activities.

As mentioned in the Introduction, The IIA Research Foundation is creating a data base of 100 organizations that are interested in periodically providing internships in internal auditing. There is obviously no year-to-year commitment since these decisions are impacted by many factors such as budgets, audit demand, and recruiting status. One way to expedite the search process is to request to be included in this data base. Internships provide organizations with the opportunity to look at students from programs that they might not otherwise consider. A student may have an excellent resume, grade point average, good recommendations, and so forth, but may be in a program from which the organization does not normally recruit. In this kind of situation, the organization may "risk" taking on an intern rather than hiring a permanent employee.

The IIA supports internship programs through its Endorsed Internal Auditing Programs. Currently, 26 schools are officially endorsed and most of them have active structured internship programs. These Endorsed Programs require schools to offer a minimum of two courses in internal auditing. A tremendous advantage of selecting interns from these schools is that the students start the internship with a knowledge of internal auditing and an appreciation of the profession.

The following statistics from Table 11 (see page 44) emphasize the advantages of recruiting from an IIA Endorsed Program:

- 74 percent of the practitioners rated a student with one internal auditing course superior to other interns.
- 98 percent of the practitioners agreed that the internal auditing course was beneficial in job performance.
- 73 percent of the practitioners felt that internal auditing courses would impact training and supervision costs.

- 79 percent of the practitioners were more receptive to hiring interns after evaluating students who took an internal auditing course

The Endorsed Programs also specify a faculty advisor to assist in coordinating aspects of the selection process. Appendix D contains a listing of the Endorsed Programs, including the faculty advisor and type of program. Often, these programs contain not only accounting majors, but all business disciplines as well as a variety of technical areas (law, engineering, computer science, etc.).

The Endorsed Programs provide the best cost/benefit approach for selecting interns. The IIA ARC also has a list of 60 "participating schools" that offer one course in internal auditing. These schools provide a good starting point for the selection process.

Results from the LSU questionnaires indicate that 53 percent of the practitioners raised their opinions (pre-internship versus post-internship) of the interns while only four percent lowered their opinions. One possible interpretation is that students who take an internal auditing course perform higher than expected.

On-site Campus Visit

Following a review of student resumes, most organizations visit campus to interview prospective interns. In over 60 percent of the programs, interns were hired on the basis of interviews (Lowe, 1965). The sponsoring organization can use the on-campus visit to maintain a visible presence on campus and to interact with students.

The organization should send material that describes the organization and the internship positions to the school's faculty advisor and placement personnel. Such information would include annual reports, internal auditing brochures, and position descriptions. The faculty advisor can distribute this material to interested students, or make it available in the placement office. The organization should also notify the faculty and provide position description forms. The forms should include relevant criteria such as type of major, grade point averages, and experience requirements. The faculty advisor or placement office can send the organization the resumes of qualified individuals so that they may pre-screen and select students for on-campus interviews.

Following a review of the resumes, the organization should contact the faculty advisor to set up an interview date and arrange a schedule. The organization or the faculty advisor can notify the placement office of the arrangements. The sponsoring organization must also inform their human resource department when appropriate.

When arranging the interview schedule, the organization should attempt to allow time for lunch with the faculty advisor and/or students. If possible the organization may choose to make a presentation to an internal auditing class or, if not offered, an auditing class. Such presentations can stimulate student interest by providing them with information about the organization as well as the profession. Also, if students have some knowledge of the organization before the interview, the limited interview time can be better spent on getting to know the student.

The interviewer should discuss typical internship arrangements and assignments to give the student an idea of what the experience will be like. There should be adequate time for the student to ask any questions he or she might have.

Following the interviews, the interviewer may want to discuss some of the students' qualifications with the faculty advisor who may be able to provide insight that the interviewer could not get from the interview process. The interviewer may also provide some feedback to the faculty advisor about how students are doing in the interview process which may help students to improve their interview skills. Post-interview sessions with interviewers provide a wealth of information to the faculty advisor relative to student attributes. After several of these sessions, the faculty advisor can form a consensus composite of the perceptions created by specific students.

The on-site campus visit gives the sponsoring organization the opportunity to evaluate students and make an impact on campus. If properly instituted, the organization, the students, and the faculty advisor can all benefit from the on-site campus interview.

Follow-up

The completion of the interview does not signal the end of the recruiting process. The recruiting organization should follow up with students and the faculty advisor to maximize the benefits derived from the recruiting process. During the interview, the interviewer must be clear about when and how the organization will select a student for the internship position. The interviewer should request transcripts for those students in which he or she is the most interested. Sometimes an organization prefers to review the transcripts of all the students interviewed. When this is the case, the request should be specified on the placement forms and the faculty advisor should be notified before the interview so that students will know to bring their transcripts to the interview. This expedites the selection process by eliminating the time it takes for students to forward transcripts to the organization after the interview.

There are several ways an organization can announce its decision regarding an intern. It can send a letter of rejection or one making an offer, which is traditional in recruiting permanent employees. However, to simplify the paperwork associated with recruiting interns, rejection letters may be eliminated. This is standard policy with several of the Endorsed Programs and is understood by the students. Alternatively, the organization may only contact the faculty advisor who may then notify the students about the decisions of various sponsors so that they can respond. Stipulations of the internship such as time, compensation, medical examinations, and any relocation arrangements should be discussed when the student calls to accept the offer. Of course, both the organization and the student should follow up the discussion with the appropriate correspondence.

The organization should inform the faculty advisor before extending an offer to a student. If an organization's first choice has already accepted another position, the faculty advisor can communicate this information. This allows the organization to make an offer to their second choice without the student realizing that he or she was not their first choice. The faculty advisor is in a better position to help both the recruiters and the students if the necessary information is forthright. This communication link has certainly been efficient and effective with The IIA's Endorsed Programs. The interview is only a part of the recruiting process. Organizations should be aware that the actions following the interviews are also significant to recruiting efforts.

The organization should ensure that all students feel they have been treated properly. Students talk to each other and share their experiences when making career decisions, selecting employers, and eliminating organizations from their potential interview lists. Future recruiting efforts could be hindered by negative publicity about the treatment students receive. Furthermore, the faculty advisor can provide informal feedback to the organization based on interviews with students.

Following the internship, the organization should maintain communication with its interns, particularly if they are interested in hiring them after graduation. This will let the students know the organization is interested and also keep the employer's name fresh in their minds.

Office Visit

The office visit is an opportunity for the student and the sponsoring organization to learn more about each other. It allows members of the organization who did not participate in the initial interview to meet and talk with the student. It also permits discussion to extend beyond the time constraint imposed by many placement offices. The student can learn a great deal about an organization during the office visit. It is important for the organization to create a good impression so that when the student returns to school, communication to peers and faculty members will be positive.

To maximize the positive impression made on the student, office visits must be structured and organized. A packet of information should be sent to the student approximately one week before the office visit. This information should contain a schedule of activities and a listing of the people the student will be meeting. It may also include information about an organization's particular interviewing techniques and the questions most commonly asked. This gives the student some preparation time that will certainly be appreciated.

Beginning the interview with a warm welcome from a few of the new staff members will break the ice and make the student more comfortable. If the student is flying in from another city, someone from the organization should meet the plane and make sure the student gets to the hotel. The arrangements for hotel accommodations and transportation to and from the office should also be made so as to minimize out-of-pocket expenses for the student. Students often do not have the financial resources to use a reimbursement system. Information relating to this should be included in the packet mailed to the student.

A variety of people should be on the interview schedule, including some who do not work in the auditing department. This is designed to provide a fresh perspective for both the organization and the student. Lunch can be scheduled with some new staff members who can answer any questions the student may not have been comfortable asking management. Another courtesy would be to include a tour of the facilities.

At the conclusion of the visit, the student should be informed of the organization's decision process, as well as a time period in which to expect an answer. It is important that the organization adheres to this time period.

Classroom Follow-up

The benefits of an internship to the individual student have been addressed in some detail. After completing the internship, the student should return to school with valuable knowledge that can also benefit other students. The faculty advisor can help in this area by requiring student presentations on internship experiences. Each intern should prepare a written report and a class presentation. Slides, overhead transparencies, handouts, and other visual aids should be used to provide clarity as well as capture the audience's attention.

The student should be given the presentation assignment before starting the internship so that the necessary information can be gathered and visual aids can be prepared. Such presentations will help those students who did not participate in an internship by allowing them to hear about the experiences of others. Students who did participate in an internship will also benefit by learning about the experiences of other interns. They will be able to compare and contrast their experiences with those of their classmates.

The presentations should address the structure of the organization, the audits that the student worked on, and the auditing approaches and techniques employed by the organization. The student should also describe the culture of the organization and its auditing philosophy. The general perceptions of the student in regard to his or her experience can help other students learn about internal auditing and make more informed career decisions (such as what type of industry might be of interest). Along with these benefits, students will also be working on presentation skills and can benefit from critiques by the instructor and their classmates.

Academic Impact of Internships

Introduction

Interviews with students and prior research indicate that internships enhance the classroom learning process. The academic course work is supplemented by exposure to the realities of the profession. Internships add a certain vitality to the classroom that is not typically reflected in textbooks. Additionally, interns are exposed to current auditing techniques and philosophies. The education process is embellished when students have an opportunity to experience some of the realities of their career selection. According to Lowe's research, a majority of former interns indicated that the internship clarified areas of theory they studied and made some courses more meaningful (Lowe, 1965). The research also showed that many interns believed that properly organized and conducted internship programs were more valuable than an equal number of additional classroom instruction. It is likely that students return to the classroom with an improved understanding of auditing theory after participating in an internship program.

Internships appear to have a differential impact on subsequent academic performance. Surveys and research indicate that the courses most impacted are auditing and audit-related (Sumners and Apostolou, 1988). It is logical for performance to improve in those courses where internship knowledge would apply. Research by Knechel and Snowball (1987) provides evidence "that students with auditing internships find their experiences and new knowledge to be of direct benefit in mastering the material presented in formal auditing courses." The obvious result of this is improved performance and grades.

The research by Koehler also indicates that students have a tendency to improve academically after an internship, which is demonstrated by an increase in grade point averages. The internship compliments the learning process, thus allowing students to better evaluate the relevance of their education and career objectives.

Another advantage of an internship is that students become more aware of the value of both written and oral communications skills. Therefore, courses such as speech, communications, and English may have more appeal after an internship experience. For example, one specific area that receives additional consideration is a foreign language. Internships in industry expose students to the international side of business and the related challenges.

In addition to the academic benefit, internships often provide motivation and direction. The additional motivation is enhanced by a welcomed break from the academic schedule and recognition of the interrelationship between course work and the professional career path. Often the motivation can be more focused if the student had a particularly satisfying internship which clarified his or her career goals.

Post-internship Evaluations

Students in the LSU program are required to complete a "Post-internship Evaluation" after their internship (see Appendix C: Internal Auditing Internship Program — Post-internship Evaluation). Data that relates to five questions has been collected for six years (N = 133) and is summarized in Table 1 using the following scale:

Scale	
1	Strongly Disagree
2	
3	Neutral
4	
5	Strongly Agree

By way of reference, the preliminary results of this survey (two years of data) were reported in 1988 (Sumners and Apostolou).

Table 1
Post-internship Evaluations

(1) Because of the internship, I feel that I will be able to make a more intelligent career decision.

Average Score	Student Classification
4.6	Undergraduate
4.7	Graduate

(2) Because of the internship, I feel that I will receive more job offers.

Average Score	Student Classification
4.1	Undergraduate
4.5	Graduate

(3) Because of the intership, I feel that I will receive better job offers.

Average Score	Student Classification
4.3	Undergraduate
4.4	Graduate

(4) Because of the internship, I feel that I will have a head start in the work environment.

Average Score	Student Classification
4.5	Undergraduate
4.6	Graduate

(5) Because of the internship, my academic courses now have more meaning.

Average Score	Student Classification
3.7	Undergraduate
4.3	Graduate

In general, students perceived that the internships were beneficial for both academic and career issues. Interestingly, the scores between undergraduate and graduate students were relatively similar except for question #5. Undergraduate students perceived less subsequent benefit in academic courses. One possible explanation for this variation is that undergraduate accounting majors tend to understand the internal auditing profession better than graduates from a variety of other disciplines (engineering, law, computer science, and so forth). The internship is more of an introduction to internal auditing for the graduate students. This is true even though the graduate students are typically more mature and have more work experience. Intuitively, the internships would be viewed as more beneficial for undergraduates; however, graduate students perceived more benefit on all issues.

Executive Summary of Summer Internship Questionnaires

Tables 2, 3, and 4 present a brief summary of the data obtained from analyzing the questionnaires in Appendices A and B. The ranked means indicate areas where students seemed to score quite well, and those where they did not. It is interesting to note that of the top scores many relate to personal qualifications, indicating that in general the interns possessed good personal characteristics. The low overall scores on performance qualifications are perhaps attributable to the comparison of students to experienced staff members — the skills listed there are certainly difficult to acquire in the classroom setting.

Even more revealing is an analysis of the correlations between the scores and the pre/post-internship evaluations. First, note from Table 3 that Performance Qualifications dominate the pre-internship correlations. At first, this makes intuitive sense since performance in their course work is relatively easy to evaluate and employers often use grade point average as a first pass cut-off tool. However, Table 3 reveals that the highest correlation is between Documentation and pre-internship evaluations. How do employers evaluate Documentation skills before interns are hired? We suspect that Documentation may be correlated with some omitted variable.

Since many in education and internal auditing are stressing writing skills, it may be that students who write well tend to impress faculty members; therefore, the faculty may overemphasize writing skills in conveying student qualifications to employers. The second and third highest correlations could also lead toward impressing the faculty. Again, please note that we are speculating because the highest correlation is unobservable at the pre-hire point, and thus must be surrogating for some other variable.

It is also interesting to compare the rankings of the correlations in the pre-internship evaluation with those in the post-internship evaluation. In particular, note that the Documentation skill that rated highest is now near the bottom (30th out of 38) as is the Elimination of Nonessentials (34th out of 38). Of the top five pre-internship correlations, none are in the top five post-internship correlations. Of the top 10 pre-internship correlations, three are in the top 10 post-internship correlations. This suggests that the skills which lead to pre-internship evaluation (and possibly to new hires as well since similar processes are used to recruit and select interns) are quite different from those skills that impress employers in the post-internship evaluation. This should suggest to employers that they may be emphasizing the wrong skills in selecting recruits.

Accepting that the ability to "Accept Responsibility" is hard to distinguish between being a Personal and Professional qualification, Table 4 is dominated by Personal qualifications. The top correlation is the one mentioned above, but the next four are all personal, and seven of the top 10 correlations are Personal. As noted before, it is interesting that the correlations here do not match well with the pre-internship correlations. Even though students scored well

Table 2
Mean Scores of Items and Correlations with Evaluations: Sorted by Mean Scores

Qualification	Item	Description	Mean	Pre-internship Correlations Rank	Pre-internship Correlations Corr.	Post-internship Correlations Rank	Post-internship Correlations Corr.
Personal	14	Attitude	4.57	34	0.24704	18	0.63202
Personal	13	Integrity	4.54	23	0.30833	35	0.52251
Professional	1	Accept Responsibility	4.53	27	0.29832	1	0.72324
Personal	1	Appearance	4.53	38	0.19019	37	0.42701
Personal	2	Conduct	4.51	32	0.26666	36	0.51431
Professional	2	Ability to Follow Instructions	4.49	31	0.27628	6	0.66813
Personal	3	Personality	4.49	20	0.32172	3	0.68066
Personal	6	Energy	4.45	37	0.21543	25	0.60825
Professional	5	Association with People	4.42	25	0.30690	28	0.59057
Professional	3	Inquisitiveness	4.39	35	0.22391	20	0.62848
Performance	5	Gaining Respect of Associates	4.38	26	0.30131	11	0.65789
Personal	4	Poise	4.36	13	0.34044	5	0.66878
Personal	8	Initiative	4.35	36	0.21683	27	0.60646
Performance	4	Communication with Supervisor	4.35	28	0.29116	24	0.61314
Personal	7	Stability	4.33	19	0.32556	4	0.67660
Professional	6	Professionalism	4.30	4	0.38872	12	0.65739
Personal	15	Confidence	4.29	15	0.33740	33	0.53844
Personal	5	Tact	4.22	17	0.33572	13	0.65460
Performance	11	Logic	4.22	11	0.34521	19	0.62997
Performance	9	Handwriting	4.21	33	0.24758	38	0.28080
Performance	8	Accuracy	4.21	21	0.31838	31	0.55170
Performance	1	Efficient Administration of Assignment	4.19	16	0.33620	14	0.64583
Performance	7	Completion within Time Frame	4.18	22	0.31155	10	0.65926
Performance	6	Meeting Deadlines	4.17	29	0.29009	29	0.56904
Performance	3	Relaring Work to Objectives	4.16	14	0.33798	15	0.64217
Personal	11	Maturity	4.13	12	0.34242	8	0.66608
Performance	2	Resourcefulness	4.13	18	0.33371	17	0.63533
Performance	10	Completeness	4.12	6	0.38300	22	0.62651
Professional	7	Effectiveness of Expression	4.11	24	0.30691	16	0.63952
Performance	16	Knowledge and Application	4.11	10	0.35313	23	0.61577
Performance	14	Documentation	4.10	1	0.41354	30	0.56055
Performance	15	Practical Solutions or Suggestions	4.07	3	0.39883	7	0.66725
Personal	10	Judgment	4.06	8	0.37232	9	0.66391
Professional	4	Creativeness	4.04	30	0.28037	26	0.60795
Performance	13	Conciseness	4.01	5	0.38856	32	0.54862
Personal	9	Decisiveness	4.00	9	0.36138	21	0.62796
Personal	12	Leadership	3.97	7	0.38283	2	0.70312
Performance	12	Elimination of Nonessentials	3.89	2	0.39924	34	0.53086

Table 3
Mean Scores of Items and Correlations with Evaluations: Sorted by Correlations with Pre-internship Evaluations

Qualification	Item	Description	Mean	Pre-internship Correlations Rank	Pre-internship Correlations Corr.	Post-internship Correlations Rank	Post-internship Correlations Corr.
Performance	14	Documentation	4.10	1	0.41354	30	0.56055
Performance	12	Elimination of Nonessentials	3.89	2	0.39924	34	0.53086
Performance	15	Practical Solutions or Suggestions	4.07	3	0.39883	7	0.66725
Professional	6	Professionalism	4.30	4	0.38872	12	0.65739
Performance	13	Conciseness	4.01	5	0.38856	32	0.54862
Performance	10	Completeness	4.12	6	0.38300	22	0.62651
Personal	12	Leadership	3.97	7	0.38283	2	0.70312
Personal	10	Judgment	4.06	8	0.37232	9	0.66391
Personal	9	Decisiveness	4.00	9	0.36138	21	0.62796
Performance	16	Knowledge and Application	4.11	10	0.35313	23	0.61577
Performance	11	Logic	4.22	11	0.34521	19	0.62997
Personal	11	Maturity	4.13	12	0.34242	8	0.66608
Personal	4	Poise	4.36	13	0.34044	5	0.66878
Performance	3	Relating Work to Objectives	4.16	14	0.33798	15	0.64217
Personal	15	Confidence	4.29	15	0.33740	33	0.53844
Performance	1	Efficient Administration of Assignment	4.19	16	0.33620	14	0.64583
Personal	5	Tact	4.22	17	0.33572	13	0.65460
Performance	2	Resourcefulness	4.13	18	0.33371	17	0.63533
Personal	7	Stability	4.33	19	0.32556	4	0.67660
Personal	3	Personality	4.49	20	0.32172	3	0.68066
Performance	8	Accuracy	4.21	21	0.31838	31	0.55170
Performance	7	Completion within Time Frame	4.18	22	0.31155	10	0.65926
Personal	13	Integrity	4.54	23	0.30833	35	0.52251
Professional	7	Effectiveness of Expression	4.11	24	0.30691	16	0.63952
Professional	5	Association with People	4.42	25	0.30690	28	0.59057
Performance	5	Gaining Respect of Associates	4.38	26	0.30131	11	0.65789
Professional	1	Accept Responsibility	4.53	27	0.29832	1	0.72324
Performance	4	Communication with Supervisor	4.35	28	0.29116	24	0.61314
Performance	6	Meeting Deadlines	4.17	29	0.29009	29	0.56904
Professional	4	Creativeness	4.04	30	0.28037	26	0.60795
Professional	2	Ability to Follow Instructions	4.49	31	0.27628	6	0.66813
Personal	2	Conduct	4.51	32	0.26666	36	0.51431
Performance	9	Handwriting	4.21	33	0.24758	38	0.28080
Personal	14	Attitude	4.57	34	0.24704	18	0.63202
Professional	3	Inquisitiveness	4.39	35	0.22391	20	0.62848
Personal	8	Initiative	4.35	36	0.21683	27	0.60646
Personal	6	Energy	4.45	37	0.21543	25	0.60825
Personal	1	Appearance	4.53	38	0.19019	37	0.42701

Table 4
Mean Scores of Items and Correlations with Evaluations: Sorted by Correlations with Post-internship Evaluations

Qualification	Item	Description	Mean	Pre-internship Correlations Rank	Pre-internship Correlations Corr.	Post-internship Correlations Rank	Post-internship Correlations Corr.
Professional	1	Accept Responsibility	4.53	27	0.29832	1	0.72324
Personal	12	Leadership	3.97	7	0.38283	2	0.70312
Personal	3	Personality	4.49	20	0.32172	3	0.68066
Personal	7	Stability	4.33	19	0.32556	4	0.67660
Personal	4	Poise	4.36	13	0.34044	5	0.66878
Professional	2	Ability to Follow Instructions	4.49	31	0.27628	6	0.66813
Performance	15	Practical Solutions or Suggestions	4.07	3	0.39883	7	0.66725
Personal	11	Maturity	4.13	12	0.34242	8	0.66608
Personal	10	Judgment	4.06	8	0.37232	9	0.66391
Performance	7	Completion within Time Frame	4.18	22	0.31155	10	0.65926
Performance	5	Gaining Respect of Associates	4.38	26	0.30131	11	0.65789
Professional	6	Professionalism	4.30	4	0.38872	12	0.65739
Personal	5	Tact	4.22	17	0.33572	13	0.65460
Performance	1	Efficient Administration of Assignment	4.19	16	0.33620	14	0.64583
Performance	3	Relating Work to Objectives	4.16	14	0.33798	15	0.64217
Professional	7	Effectiveness of Expression	4.11	24	0.30691	16	0.63952
Performance	2	Resourcefulness	4.13	18	0.33371	17	0.63533
Personal	14	Attitude	4.57	34	0.24704	18	0.63202
Performance	11	Logic	4.22	11	0.34521	19	0.62997
Professional	3	Inquisitiveness	4.39	35	0.22391	20	0.62848
Personal	9	Decisiveness	4.00	9	0.36138	21	0.62796
Performance	10	Completeness	4.12	6	0.38300	22	0.62651
Performance	16	Knowledge and Application	4.11	10	0.35313	23	0.61577
Performance	4	Communication with Supervisor	4.35	28	0.29116	24	0.61314
Personal	6	Energy	4.45	37	0.21543	25	0.60825
Professional	4	Creativeness	4.04	30	0.28037	26	0.60795
Personal	8	Initiative	4.35	36	0.21683	27	0.60646
Professional	5	Association with People	4.42	25	0.30690	28	0.59057
Performance	6	Meeting Deadlines	4.17	29	0.29009	29	0.56904
Performance	14	Documentation	4.10	1	0.41354	30	0.56055
Performance	8	Accuracy	4.21	21	0.31838	31	0.55170
Performance	13	Conciseness	4.01	5	0.38856	32	0.54862
Personal	15	Confidence	4.29	15	0.33740	33	0.53844
Performance	12	Elimination of Nonessentials	3.89	2	0.39924	34	0.53086
Personal	13	Integrity	4.54	23	0.30833	35	0.52251
Personal	2	Conduct	4.51	32	0.26666	36	0.51431
Personal	1	Appearance	4.53	38	0.19019	37	0.42701
Performance	9	Handwriting	4.21	33	0.24758	38	0.28080

on many personal skills, there are clear differences in some of these skills that seem to impress employers. In particular, this analysis suggests that employers should pay much more attention to the students' ability to accept responsibility and follow instructions.

This rather simplistic correlation analysis was supplemented with factor analysis which provided similar results. The three factors were labeled Performance Qualifications, Professional Qualifications, and Personal Qualifications. In the pre-internship evaluations, the performance skills factor had a much stronger correlation with good scores than the other factors, but in the post-internship evaluations management skills had the highest correlation. These results support the interpretation given above, and support the assertion that employers may be directing their efforts in the wrong areas. More attention needs to be made to better identify those who will succeed, and success is not related to performance skills nor to the personal skills as currently measured.

Ancillary Issues

The questionnaire contained other items of interest, such as whether or not the employer perceived that the intern was or was not interested in permanent employment, whether or not the evaluator would recommend permanent employment, and whether or not the evaluator planned to discuss the evaluation with the intern. These results are shown in Table 5 on page 38 and Tables 6 and 7 on page 39.

As would be expected, the means for the interns who the evaluators would recommend for permanent employment were substantially higher than for those who would not be recommended. Even given the small sample size of those not recommended, the difference is statistically significant at any reasonable level (by application of the independent sample t test; $t^* = 9.38$ with seven degrees of freedom). There was no statistically significant difference among the groups based on the level of the intern's perceived interest in employment.

Perhaps the most telling of the ancillary analysis regards the plans to discuss the evaluation. It is quite apparent that the evaluators gave lower scores when they did not intend to discuss the evaluation with the intern ($t^* = 4.63$ with 40 degrees of freedom). The question arises as to the nature and cause of this difference, and more importantly whether or not the evaluators were influenced by this decision. The classic question cannot be answered: Which came first, the chicken or the egg? Did the evaluators choose not to convey bad information, or did they give lower evaluations because they were not going to discuss the results? Either answer is inappropriate for the work environment. Interns, and employees in general, need constructive feedback so that corrective action can be taken. Thus, if evaluators are avoiding conveying bad news, this is not beneficial. It seems obvious that evaluators should not give lower evaluations just because they will not have to face the intern. Extending the line of reasoning would yield the scenario where the evaluator gave higher evaluations simply to make the discussions more pleasant.

Table 5
Means by Ancillary Class Variables
(Permanent Employment Decision)

Panel A - Question #2 (Form E). Would you recommend that your company consider this student for permanent employment?

PERM	N Obs	Variable	N	Mean	Std Dev
NO	7	PRE	6	3.50000	0.54772
		POST	7	3.14286	0.37796
		DIFF	6	-0.33333	0.51640
YES	160	PRE	134	3.88657	0.69215
		POST	160	4.54312	0.55043
		DIFF	134	0.65746	0.61685
UNKNOWN	20	PRE	17	3.42353	0.70669
		POST	20	3.72000	0.70904
		DIFF	17	0.42353	0.85112

Comments:
While 96 percent of the respondents would consider their intern for permanent employment, four percent would not. For those that would consider the intern for permanent employment the post-intern mean of 4.5 on a scale of 1-5 increased from a pre-internship mean of 3.9. In contrast, for those that would not consider their intern for a permanent position the post-intern mean of 3.1 decreased from a pre-intern mean of 3.5. There are several messages from this data. Obviously, a longer evaluation period significantly impacted the evaluation. Internships provide additional information for better hiring decisions.

Table 6
Means by Ancillary Class Variables
(Interest in Permanent Employment)

Panel B - Question #3. Do you perceive that the student is interested in permanent employment with your company?

INTER					
NO	25	PRE	21	3.90476	0.62488
		POST	25	4.08000	0.75939
		DIFF	21	0.23810	0.76842
YES	91	PRE	77	3.81818	0.72124
		POST	91	4.42308	0.62505
		DIFF	77	0.61688	0.58746
UNKNOWN	61	PRE	51	3.74510	0.71675
		POST	61	4.37377	0.71319
		DIFF	51	0.62353	0.77216

Table 7
Means by Ancillary Class Variables
(Discussion of Evaluation)

Panel C - Question #4. Do you plan to discuss this evaluation with the student?

DISCUSS					
NO	31	PRE	28	3.85714	0.65060
		POST	31	3.90323	0.70023
		DIFF	28	0.14286	0.65060
YES	150	PRE	127	3.85827	0.71007
		POST	150	4.53000	0.61478
		DIFF	127	0.65748	0.65846

Comments:
Note that there is a positive correlation between post-intern evaluations and the decisions to discuss the evaluations. Practitioners discussed the evaluations more often with students with higher evaluations than with students with lower evaluations. Perhaps we all prefer to deliver good news. Also, practitioners may be slightly more reluctant to provide bad news to temporary interns than to permanent employees. Obviously, public relations with the student and the school might impact the decision not to convey the evaluation results.

Question 1-D from Appendix A asks for an overall evaluation as follows:

Scale
5 - Excellent
4 - Good
3 - Average
2 - Below Average
1 - Poor

____ Overall evaluation of student *before* summer internship.
____ Overall evaluation of student *after* summer internship.

The changes in the ratings were as follows:

Number of Responses	Percent	Evaluation Scale Increase (Decrease)
6	4	(1)
67	43	0
72	46	1
11	7	2
156	100	

The results of this data are rather significant. Only four percent of the practitioners lowered their evaluation while 53 percent have a higher evaluation of the particular student after the internship. The interpretation of this data is subject to conjecture. Perhaps one possible explanation is that interns with an academic background in internal auditing perform at a higher level than anticipated.

Tables 8, 9, and 10 present the professional, performance, and personal qualifications by mean rankings (5 = excellent, 1 = poor). Table 11 on page 44 presents a recap of the balance of the responses to the survey provided by the organization.

Table 8
Professional Qualifications Ranked by Means

Professional Qualifications	Mean	Std. Dev.
Ability to accept responsibility	4.52798	0.63150
Ability to follow instructions	4.48705	0.63212
Aptitude for associating with people	4.41762	0.66583
Inquisitiveness	4.39275	0.66053
Professionalism	4.30311	0.73456
Effectiveness of expression	4.10524	0.70567
Creativeness	4.04219	0.69096

Comments:
The students were ranked relatively high on all of the qualifications. Creativeness was ranked the lowest, which would probably be expected for an intern. There is, however, a message for students and educators—internal auditing is a profession that requires creativeness in solving unstructured problems. To the extent possible, classroom assignments should mirror "real world" scenarios.

Table 9
Performance Qualifications Ranked by Means

Performance Qualifications	Mean	Std. Dev.
Gaining respect of associates	4.38125	0.69986
Communication with supervisor	4.35393	0.71132
Logic	4.22396	0.67634
Legible handwriting	4.21053	0.83912
Accuracy	4.20990	0.68732
Efficient administration of assignment	4.19424	0.65141
Effective completion of assignment within time allocated	4.17927	0.76129
Meeting scheduled deadlines	4.16528	0.71260
Relating work to objectives	4.16477	0.71151
Resourcefulness in assignment	4.12552	0.71266
Completeness	4.12124	0.66826
Knowledge and application	4.10785	0.73255
Documentation	4.09635	0.69797
Practical solutions or suggestions	4.07187	0.73309
Conciseness	4.00677	0.69697
Elimination of nonessentials	3.88639	0.69708

Comments:
The last few items in the table above are clearly attributes that are best acquired on the job. The academic community should address these items but they are too situation-specific for the classroom.

Table 10
Personal Qualifications Ranked by Means

Personal Qualifications	Mean	Std. Dev.
Attitude	4.56943	0.64787
Integrity	4.54301	0.56841
Appearance	4.52642	0.64208
Conduct	4.51347	0.62226
Personality	4.49326	0.61059
Energy	4.44922	0.65853
Poise	4.35699	0.70109
Initiative	4.34663	0.76124
Stability	4.33472	0.66910
Confidence	4.29326	0.70954
Tact	4.21554	0.74866
Maturity	4.12746	0.81049
Judgment	4.06477	0.67098
Decisiveness	3.99741	0.72467
Leadership	3.97414	0.74156

Comments:
Students enrolled in a IIA Endorsed Internal Auditing Program should have a good attitude and understand the importance of integrity to the profession. These attributes are accordingly ranked high in the above table. Intuitively, one might expect interns to score lower on maturity, judgment, decisiveness, and leadership.

Table 11
Responses to Questions 5–12
(Form E, Appendix A)

Questions	Response		Percent	Mean
5. How would you evaluate this student (who has had one internal auditing course) to other students that you hire for summer work?	101	Superior	74	
	30	Same Level	22	
	6	Below	4	.569
6. Do you feel that the internal auditing course was beneficial to the student in his or her job?	187	Yes	98	
	3	No	2	.984
7. Do you feel that hiring a student who has taken an auditing course would impact your training or supervision costs?	138	Yes	73	
	51	No	27	.730
8. Do you feel that hiring a student with 12 hours of internal auditing would significantly reduce your training and supervision costs?	121	Yes	65	
	64	No	35	.654
9. Has your experience with the LSU Internal Auditing Pilot School or this particular student made you more receptive to hiring students as opposed to experienced persons?	133	Yes	79	
	35	No	21	.791
10. Do you feel that The Institute of Internal Auditors should aggressively encourage internal auditing education at colleges and universities?	185	Yes	98	
	3	No	2	.984
11. Are you interested in participating in the internship program next year?	176	Yes	99	
	2	No	1	.989
12. What type of interviewing format do you prefer?	86	On-campus interviews	48	
	52	On campus with selected office visits	29	
	16	Office visits only	8	
	20	Faculty recommendations	11	
	7	Review of resumes	4	

Comments:

(1) The means were calculated by assigning a "1" to the first choice and a "0" to the last choice (i.e., yes = 1, no = 0).

(2) The number of responses to the above questions vary due to non-responses on selected questions.

(3) On Question #12, 89 percent of the respondents had multiple responses. The first selection is reflected in the above response.

Conclusion

Internships are of significant benefit to the profession, the school, the student, and the organization. An integral part of an internship program is the development and implementation of the appropriate structure. Commitment by everyone involved is an important part of the process.

Research indicates that internships have a positive academic impact. This is important because academic relations play a significant role in the future of the internal auditing profession. As the profession matures and meets the challenges of the 21st century, it is necessary to recruit the best and brightest students to the profession. Internships serve as a cost-effective recruiting tool in meeting this challenge.

The IIA's motto is "Progress Through Sharing." In keeping with this motto, internships provide an excellent opportunity for organizations to share the internal auditing profession with universities and, more importantly, the student.

Appendix A
FORM E

Summer Internship Survey
Student Evaluation by Sponsor

CONFIDENTIAL

This document will be reviewed *only* by Glenn E. Sumners. Your candid evaluation will be appreciated.

DATA ON EVALUATOR

Date ______________________

Name ______________________

Position ______________________

Company ______________________

Address ______________________

Phone ______________________

NAME OF STUDENT ______________________

Please attach a *brief* one-page report on the type of work performed by the student that would enhance his/her professional development. Also, please attach any separate evaluation that you are required, by your company, to file on the student.

1. Please rate the student on the following items using a 5-point scale.
   5 - Excellent
   4 - Good
   3 - Average
   2 - Below Average
   1 - Poor

   A. Performance Qualifications
   _____ 1. Efficient administration of assignment
   _____ 2. Resourcefulness in assignment
   _____ 3. Relating work to objectives
   _____ 4. Communication with supervisor
   _____ 5. Gaining respect of associates
   _____ 6. Meeting scheduled deadlines
   _____ 7. Effective completion of assignment within time allocated
   _____ 8. Accuracy
   _____ 9. Legible handwriting
   _____ 10. Completeness
   _____ 11. Logic
   _____ 12. Elimination of nonessentials
   _____ 13. Conciseness
   _____ 14. Documentation
   _____ 15. Practical solutions or suggestions
   _____ 16. Knowledge and application

B. Professional Qualifications
_____ 1. Ability to accept responsibility
_____ 2. Ability to follow instructions
_____ 3. Inquisitiveness
_____ 4. Creativeness
_____ 5. Aptitude for associating with people
_____ 6. Professionalism
_____ 7. Effectiveness of expression

C. Personal Qualifications
_____ 1. Appearance
_____ 2. Conduct
_____ 3. Personally
_____ 4. Poise
_____ 5. Tact
_____ 6. Energy
_____ 7. Stability
_____ 8. Initiative
_____ 9. Decisiveness
_____ 10. Judgment
_____ 11. Maturity
_____ 12. Leadership
_____ 13. Integrity
_____ 14. Attitude
_____ 15. Confidence

D. Miscellaneous
_____ 1. Overall evaluation *before* summer internship.
_____ 2. Overall evaluation *after* summer internship

Other

2. Would you recommend that your company consider this student for permanent employment?
_____ Yes
_____ Undecided
_____ No

3. Do you perceive that the student is interested in permanent employment with your company?
_____ Yes
_____ Undecided
_____ No

4. Do you plan to discuss this evaluation with the student?
_____ Yes
_____ No

5. How would you evaluate this student (who has had one internal auditing course) to other students that you hire for summer work?
_____ Superior
_____ Same level
_____ Below

6. Do you feel that the internal auditing course was beneficial to the student in his/her job?
_____ Yes
_____ No

7. Do you feel that hiring a student who has taken an auditing course would impact your training or supervision costs?
_____ Yes
_____ No

8. Do you feel that hiring a student with twelve (12) hours of internal auditing would significantly reduce your training and supervision costs?
_____ Yes
_____ No

9. Has your experience with the LSU Internal Auditing Pilot School or this particular student made you more receptive to hiring a student as opposed to a person with more work experience?
_____ Yes
_____ No

10. Do you feel that The Institute of Internal Auditors should aggressively encourage internal auditing education at colleges and universities?
_____ Yes
_____ No

Miscellaneous

11. Are you interested in participating in the internship program next year?
_____ Yes
_____ No

12. What type of interviewing format do you prefer?
_____ On-campus interviews.
_____ On campus with selected office visits
_____ Office visits only
_____ Faculty recommendations
_____ Review of resumes

13. Please include any additional comments or suggestions that would improve the present system for placement of students in internship positions.

14. How can I assist you in the interviewing or placement process?

15. How can I help prepare the students for their internship?

16. Other Comments

Thank you for your time in completing this evaluation.

Appendix B
FORM S

To be filled out by student as course requirement. You will not be graded on your responses to this questionnaire.	CONFIDENTIAL This form will only be reviewed by the Faculty Advisor. Your candid comments will be appreciated.

Summer Internship Survey
Student Report

BIOGRAPHICAL (Print or type)

1. Name ____________________

2. Address ____________________

   ____

3. Telephone (H) ____________ (W) ____________

4. Summer Employer ____________________

5. Location ____________________

6. Name of Immediate Supervisor ____________________

   Title ____________________

   Address ____________________

   Phone ____________________

7. Classification of job position ____________________

8. Starting date of work ____________ Last day ____________

9. Average no. of hours worked per week ____________

10. Expected graduation date ____________________

11. GPA ____________ overall

    ____________ accounting

12. When will you start interviewing? ____________________

13. List the ten (10) companies/firms that you are interested in interviewing with for permanent employment.

List those you were considering before your internship	List those you are now considering
1. ____________________	1. ____________________
2. ____________________	2. ____________________
3. ____________________	3. ____________________
4. ____________________	4. ____________________
5. ____________________	5. ____________________
6. ____________________	6. ____________________
7. ____________________	7. ____________________
8. ____________________	8. ____________________
9. ____________________	9. ____________________
10. ____________________	10. ____________________

COMPENSATION

14. Starting salary ____________________ Ending salary ____________________

15. Included in insurance program? ________ Yes ________ No

16. List any other fringe benefits ____

____

____

TRAVEL

17. What percent of your work was away from the home office? __________%

18. How were you reimbursed for travel expenses?

__________ Actual expenses

__________ Per diem (if so, specify below)

__________ Meals

__________ Hotel

19. List the different cities in which you worked ______________________________

____

____

____

20. Was there a salary adjustment for travel? ______ Yes ______ No

If yes, explain: ______________________________

____

____

TRAINING

21. Indicate the composition of your audit work

______% Financial audits
______% Operational audits
______% Compliance audits
______% Management skills
______% Other
______% Other
100% Total

22. Did you have a training session other than on-the-job? ______ Yes ______ No

If yes, describe: ______________________________

____

____

23. What type of specialized on-the-job training did you receive? ______________________________

____

____

____

____

24. Were you exposed to EDP auditing? ______ Yes ______ No

    If yes, explain ____

    ____

    ____

    ____

ACADEMIC

25. How was the summer internship academically beneficial? ________________________

    ____

    ____

    ____

    ____

    ____

26. Was the first internal auditing course beneficial in your summer internship?

    ______ Yes ______ No If yes, explain:

    ____

    ____

    ____

    ____

27. Attach a two-page typed report about your summer internship to support receipt of 3 hours of university credit in lieu of course work (i.e., benefits derived from job, type of work done, professional development, etc.).

EVALUATION OF EMPLOYER

28. Do you plan to interview with your summer employer for permanent employment?

    ______ Yes ______ No

29. Do you have more or less of an interest in this company as a result of your internship?

    ______ More ______ Less

30. Assign a percent probability that you will accept a job with this company if an offer is made.

    ______%

31. Would you recommend this company for inclusion in the internal auditing summer internship next year?

    ________ Yes ________ Undecided ________ No

32. Would you recommend this company to your best friend? ________ Yes ________ No

33. Please rate the employer on the following items on a scale of 1-5 (1-outstanding, 3-average, 5-poor)
    ________ Professionalism of audit staff
    ________ Supervision
    ________ Quality of training received
    ________ General evaluation of company

34. What suggestions would you make to your employer to improve the quality of the summer internship program? ____

    ____

    ____

    ____

35. How has the internship contributed to your professional development? ____________________

    ____

    ____

    ____

36. Did you consider internal auditing as a career prior to joining the LSU program?

    ________ Yes ________ No

MISCELLANEOUS

37. Would you consider permanent employment in the city in which you worked?

    ________ Yes ________ No

38. Rank order the five cities that you would like to consider for permanent employment.

List those you were considering before your internship	List those you are now considering
1. ________________	1. ________________
2. ________________	2. ________________
3. ________________	3. ________________
4. ________________	4. ________________
5. ________________	5. ________________

39. What suggestions do you have for the faculty advisor to improve the summer internship program?

____

____

____

____

____

40. Rank order your preference for permanent employment. Select from the following list.

_______ Government

_______ Public Accounting (Local)

_______ Public Accounting (Big 8)

_______ Internal Auditing

_______ Industry (other than I/A)

_______ Education

List those you were considering before your internship	List those you are now considering
1. ________________	1. ________________
2. ________________	2. ________________
3. ________________	3. ________________
4. ________________	4. ________________
5. ________________	5. ________________

42. What impact did your summer internship have on your consideration of internal auditing as a potential career for you?

_______ Now considering it more

_______ No change

_______ Now considering it less

43. What was the most enjoyable part of the summer internship? ____________________

____

____

____

____

44. What was the least enjoyable part of the summer internship? ____________________

____

____

____

____

45. How can the internal auditing course be revised to be more beneficial to the summer internship program?

____

____

____

____

46. Please indicate below any additional comments you would like to make.

____

____

____

____

Return in enclosed envelope as soon as possible. Do not wait until the last day of work. The form is needed prior to assignment of pass/fail grade.

Appendix C

Louisiana State University
Internal Auditing Internship Program - Post-internship Evaluation

Please circle the number that best reflects your opinion relative to the LSU Internal Auditing Internship Program.

(1) Because of my internship through the Program, I feel I will be able to make a more intelligent career decision.

Strongly Disagree		Neutral		Strongly Agree
1	2	3	4	5

(2) Because of the internship I feel that I will receive more job offers.

Strongly Disagree		Neutral		Strongly Agree
1	2	3	4	5

(3) Because of the internship I feel that I will receive better job offers.

Strongly Disagree		Neutral		Strongly Agree
1	2	3	4	5

(4) Because of the internship I feel that I will have a head start in the work environment.

Strongly Disagree		Neutral		Strongly Agree
1	2	3	4	5

(5) Because of the internship my academic courses now have more meaning.

Strongly Disagree		Neutral		Strongly Agree
1	2	3	4	5

(6) Check One _______ Undergraduate _______ Graduate

DO NOT PUT YOUR NAME ON THIS FORM

Appendix D

The Institute of Internal Auditors Endorsed Internal Auditing Program 1993 Roster

Arizona State University West
4701 W. Thunderbird Road
Phoenix, AZ 85069-7100
Phone (602) 543-6200
FAX (602) 543-6220
Stanley Y. Chang, PhD, CIA, CMA
Program: Undergraduate

Bentley College
175 Forest Street
Waltham, MA 02154-4705
Phone (617) 891-2000
Priscilla A. Burnaby, PhD, CPA
Program: Undergraduate

Boise State University
Department of Accounting
1910 University Drive
Boise, ID 83725
Phone (208) 385-1261
Thomas J. English, PhD, CPA
Program: Undergraduate

Brigham Young University
School of Accountancy
531 TNRB
Provo, UT 84602
Phone (801) 378-3216
Keith R. Howe, PhD, CIA
Program: Graduate

California State University Dominguez Hills
1000 E. Victoria Street
Carson, CA 90747
Phone (310) 516-3575
Robert J. Koester, PhD
Program: Undergraduate

Clemson University
School of Accountancy
301 Sirrine Hall
Clemson, SC 29634-1303
Phone (803) 656-4888
G. Thomas Friedlob, PhD, CPA, CMA
Program: Undergraduate, Graduate

Cleveland State University
Department of Accounting
and Business Law
Cleveland, OH 44115
Phone (216) 687-3671
Heidi Hylton Meier, DBA, CPA
Program: Undergraduate, Graduate

Eastern Michigan University
Department of Accounting
406 Owen
Ypsilanti, MI 48197
Phone (313) 487-0246
D. Robert Okopny, PhD, CIA, CMA
Program: Undergraduate, Graduate

Florida Atlantic University
School of Accounting
P.O. Box 3091
Boca Raton, FL 33431-0991
Phone: (407) 367-3636
Alan H. Friedberg, PhD
Program: Graduate

Florida International University
College of Business Administration
University Park
Miami, FL 33199
Phone (305) 348-3267
Mortimer Dittenhofer, PhD, CIA
Program: Graduate

Howard University
Department of Accounting
School of Business & Public Administration
Washington, DC 20059
Phone (202) 806-1563
Horton L. Sorkin, PhD, CIA
Program: Undergraduate

King Fahd University of Petroleum and Minerals
College of Industrial Management
Department of Accounting and MIS
Dhahran 31261, Saudi Arabia
Phone (966) 03/860-2656
Kamal E. Said, PhD
Program: Undergraduate/Graduate

Louisiana State University
Accounting Department
3101 CEBA Building
Baton Rouge, LA 70803
Phone (504) 388-6210
Glenn E. Sumners, DBA, CPA
Program: Undergraduate, Graduate

New York University
48 Cooper Square
New York, NY 10003
Phone (212) 998-7190
Richard Vigilante, PhD
Program: Graduate

Norwegian School of Management
Elias Smiths vei 15
Postboks 580
N-1301 Sandrika
Norway
Phone (47) 2-47-05-00
Knut Loken
Program: Graduate

Old Dominion University
Department of Accounting
Norfolk, VA 23529-0229
Phone: (804) 683-3514
Douglas E. Ziegenfuss, PhD
Program: Undergraduate

San Francisco State University
School of Business
1600 Holloway Avenue
San Francisco, CA 94132
Phone (415) 338-6285
John O'Shaughnessy, PhD, CIA, CMA
Program: Undergraduate

Seton Hall University
W. Paul Stillman School of Business
South Orange, NJ 07079
Phone (201) 761-9239
John P. Deehan, PhD
Program: Undergraduate

Southwest Missouri State University
901 South National Ave.
Springfield, MO 65804-0094
Phone: (417) 836-5414
Michael J. Cerullo, PhD, CPA
Program: Undergraduate/Graduate

Tennessee Technological University
Department of Accounting and Finance
645 Laurel Circle, Campus Box 5024
Cookeville, TN 38501
Phone (615) 372-3885
Jon A. Booker, PhD, CIA, CPA
Program: Undergraduate, Graduate

University of Aix-Marseille III
Graduate School of Business
Clos Guiot
boulevard des Camus
13540 Puyricard
FRANCE
Phone (33) 42 92 10 50
FAX (33) 42 92 21 25
Didier Yon, PhD, CPA
Program: Graduate

University of Alabama at Birmingham
UAB School of Business
University Station
Birmingham, AL 35294
Phone (205) 934-8820
Deborah W. Tanju, PhD, CIA, CMA
Program: Undergraduate

University of Houston
Department of Accountancy and Taxation
College of Business Administration
Houston, TX 77204-6283
Phone (713) 743-4850
Jerry R. Strawser, PhD, CPA
Program: Undergraduate, Graduate

University of New Orleans
Department of Accounting
College of Business Administration
New Orleans, LA 70148
Phone (504) 286-6429
Joyce C. Lambert, PhD, CPA
Program: Undergraduate

University of North Carolina Charlotte
Belk College of Business Administration
Charlotte, NC 28223
Phone (704) 547-4405
Terry J. Nunley, PhD, CPA
Program: Undergraduate

University of North Texas
College of Business Administration
P.O. Box 13677
Denton, TX 76203-3677
Phone (817) 565-3093
Raymond J. Clay, Jr., DBA, CPA
Program: Graduate

References

"Accounting Internship Programs Provide "On-Site" Service to Students and CPAs," *The Michigan CPA* (Winter, 1984), pp. 30-31.

Ankers, Raymond G.; Jencks, William B.; Reimer, Clarence F.; Werner, M.T.; Wheeler, John T.; Zlatkovick, Charles T.; and Thompson, David W. "Report of the Committee on Internship Programs," *The Accounting Review* (July 1, 1952), pp. 316-323.

Barnett, Bruce G. "The Mentor-Intern Relationship: Making the Most of Learning from Experience," *NAASP Bulletin* (May 1990), pp. 17-24.

Beran, Denny K.; Brown, Everlyn; and Clay, Raymond J. "The Internship Program: A "Win, Win, Win" Scenario," (unpublished paper).

Berger, Jason. "Making an Internship Work," *Public Relations Journal* (April 1991), pp. 30-31.

Brenner, Vincent C. and Sumners, Glenn E. "A New Development in Internal Audit Education," *Internal Auditor* (February 1987), pp. 44-48.

Brenner, Vincent C. and Sumners, Glenn E. "Learning Internal Audit on Campus," *New Accountant* (April 1992), pp. 14-18.

Brightman, Deborah E. "How to Build An Internship Program," *Public Relations Journal* (January 1989), pp. 29-30.

Chandra, Gyan and Paperman, Jacob B. "Accounting Internships and CPA Firms," *The CPA Journal* (September 1983), pp. 75-76.

Chastain, James. "A Summer Internship – What's In It For You?," *The Black Collegian* (January/February 1990), pp. 92 and 178-179.

Committee on Accounting Personnel of the American Institute of Accountants and the Committee on Faculty Residency and Internship Programs of the American Accounting Association. "Statement of Standards and Responsibilities Under Public Accounting Internship Programs," *The Accounting Review* (April 1955), pp. 206-210.

DeFilippis, Robert A. "Internship in Small Practice Units," *The CPA Journal* (January 1982), pp. 81-82.

Edleson, Harriet. "Innovative Internships," *HR Magazine* (July 1991), pp. 39-41.

Glover, Edwin E. "A Step Beyond Theory," *Internal Auditor* (April 1982), pp. 43-45.

Goodman, Leonard. "Internship Programs: What CPA Firms Should Know," *Journal of Accountancy* (October 1982), pp. 112-114.

Hicks, Donald W. "Junior Level Interns," *Journal of Accountancy* (August 1984), p. 122.

Hicks, Donald W. "Reaching Students One-on-One," *Internal Auditor* (February 1984), pp. 27-28.

Hollingsworth, Pierce. "The Case for Interns," *FOLIO* (June 1990), pp. 131-132.

The Institute of Internal Auditors. "Guidelines for the Development of Faculty Residency and Student Internship Programs," (March 1990), pp. 3-1 – 3-21.

"Internships Give Graduates a Boost Into the "Real World," *IIA Today* (April/May 1992), p. 6.

Kimmell, Dennis L. and Kimmell, Sharon L. "Internal Auditing Internships," *Internal Auditor* (August 1988), pp. 27-30.

Knechel, W. Robert and Snowball, Doug. "Accounting Internships and Subsequent Academic Performance: An Empirical Study," *The Accounting Review* (October 1987), pp. 799-807.

Koehler, Robert W. "The Effect of Internship Programs on Subsequent College Performance," *The Accounting Review* (April 1974), pp. 382-384.

Kowalczyk, David S. "An Internship Program – A Practical Experience," *The Internal Auditor* (August 1974), pp. 50-52.

Lowe, Ross E. "Public Accounting Internships," *The Accounting Review* (October 1965), pp. 839-846.

McDaniel, Roger L. "Internships: Passport to the Corporate World." (Unpublished paper.)

Paperman, Jacob B. and Chandra, Gyan. "Administration of a Professional Practice," *The Ohio CPA Journal* (Winter 1984), pp. 47-49.

Posey, Larry O.; Carlisle, Kenneth E.; and Smellie, Donald C. "An Internship Case Study," *Training and Development Journal* (February 1988), pp. 59-64.

Ricchiute, David N. "Internships and the Local Practitioner," *Journal Accountancy* (July 1980), pp. 35-39.

Robinson, William L. "Implementing a Successful Intern Program," *Journal of Property Management* (January/February 1990), pp. 36-38.

Ruiz, Jon and VanderMeer, Steve. "Internships: High Returns on Low Investments," *Public Management* (February 1989), pp. 16-17.

Sumners, Glenn E. "Louisiana State University Internal Audit Pilot School: Report to the Advisory Board," (October 1987).

Sumners, Glenn E. "The Beneficial Impact of Internships in Internal Auditing." Report for the Education and Training Internal Auditors Colloquium (July 1988).

Sumners, Glenn E. and Apostolou, Barbara. "The Beneficial Impact of Internships in Internal Auditing," *Managerial Auditing Journal* (Volume 3, Number 3, 1988), pp. 11-14.

Organizations

(1) The National Society for Internships and Experiential Education (NSIEE) – is a professional association and national resource center that supports the use of learning through experience for:

- Intellectual development.
- Civic and social responsibility.
- Career exploration.
- Cross-cultural and global awareness.
- Ethical development.
- Personal growth.

NSIEE was founded in 1971 as the National Center for Public Service Internship Programs and the Society for Field Experience Education. The national office is in Raleigh, North Carolina.

Experiential Education includes:

- Internships.
- Community and public service-learning.
- Education.
- Field studies.
- Intercultural programs.
- Experiential learning in the classroom and outdoors.
- All forms of active learning.

NSIEE's goals are:

- To advocate for the use of experiential learning throughout the educational system and the larger community.
- To disseminate information on principles of good practice and on innovations in the field.
- To enhance the professional growth and leadership development of our members.
- To encourage the development and dissemination of research and theory related to experiential learning.

Address:

National Society for Internships and
Experiential Education
3509 Haworth Drive, Suite 207
Raleigh, North Carolina 27609

The NSIEE has published a guide called The National Directory of Internships. Its internship options range from teaching children for the Audubon Naturalist Society of the Central Atlantic States to spending 10 weeks at Hewlett-Packard in their finance, information system, or marketing divisions.

(2) The New York-based Council on International Educational Exchange (CIEE) arranges for work permits in Britain, France, Germany, New Zealand, Costa Rica, Jamaica, and Ireland. The CIEE also helps students find jobs and lodging in the country of their choice.

(3) The Institute of Internal Auditors supports internships in internal auditing through its Academic Relations Committee. For information contact:

Manager of Academic Relations
The Institute of Internal Auditors
249 Maitland Ave.
Altamonte Springs, Florida 32701
(407) 830-7600